JOHN RUTTER

GLORIA

for mixed voices with brass,
percussion, and organ

or mixed voices
and orchestra

I = pg. 1
II = pg. 15
III = pg. 24

MUSIC DEPARTMENT

OXFORD

UNIVERSITY PRESS

This work was commissioned by the Voices of Mel Olson
and first performed on 5 May 1974 in Omaha, U.S.A.,
under the direction of the composer.

Instrumentation

(a) Brass, percussion, and organ:

4 Trumpets in C
2 Tenor trombones
Bass trombone
Tuba
Timpani and percussion (2 or 3 players)
Organ

(b) Orchestra:

2.2.2.2.-4.3.3.1
Timpani, percussion, and harp
Strings

Full scores and instrumental parts for both versions are on hire.

A vocal score of the first movement of this work is available separately.

Hardback full scores for both the full orchestra and brass and organ
versions of this work, as well as all performing material for the latter
version, are also available for purchase.

Duration 17 minutes

for Mel Olson

GLORIA

John Rutter

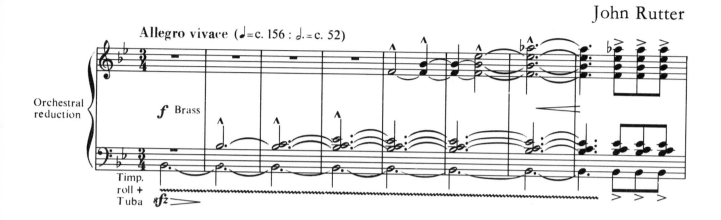

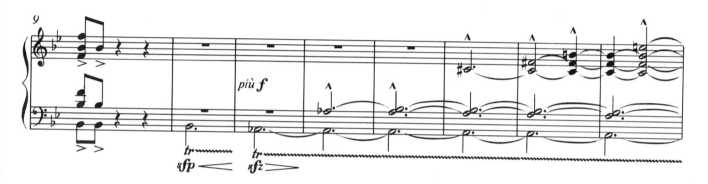

Printed in Great Britain
OXFORD UNIVERSITY PRESS, MUSIC DEPARTMENT, GREAT CLARENDON STREET, OXFORD OX2 6DP

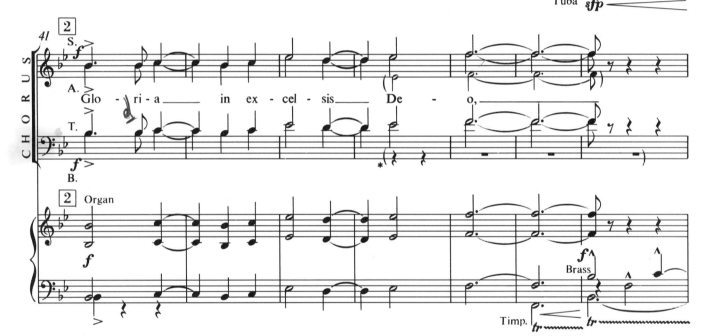

*Basses may omit these two notes

in ex - cel - sis____ De - o.____

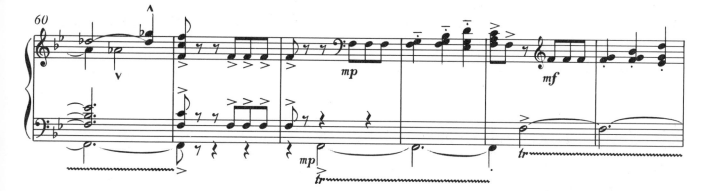

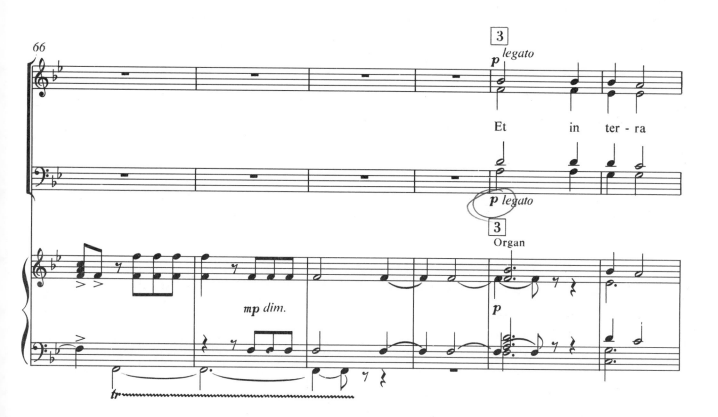

Et in ter - ra

pax_____ ho -

pax ho - mi - ni - bus bo - nae vo - lun - ta - tis.

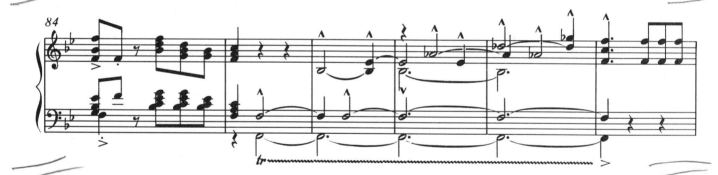

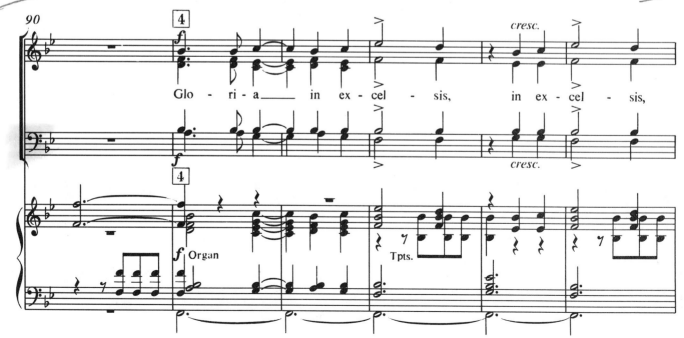

Glo - ri - a_____ in ex - cel - sis, in ex - cel - sis,

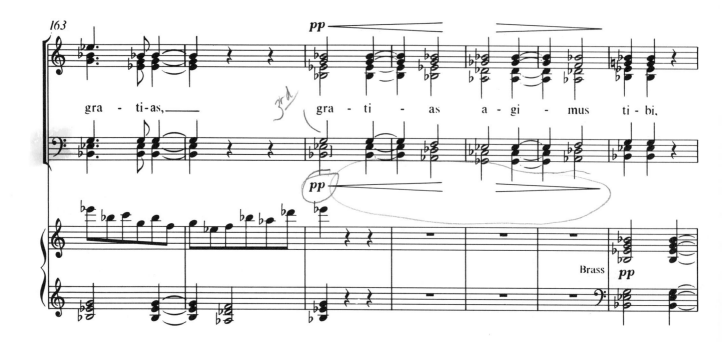

gra - ti - as a - gi - mus ti - bi

Organ   *p*

cresc.   *mp cresc.*   *mf cresc.*

+ Tenors

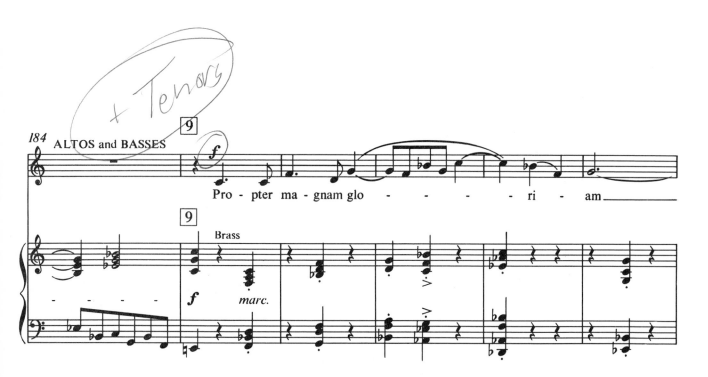

ALTOS and BASSES   **9**   *f*

Pro - pter ma - gnam glo - - - ri - am _____

9   Brass

f   *marc.*

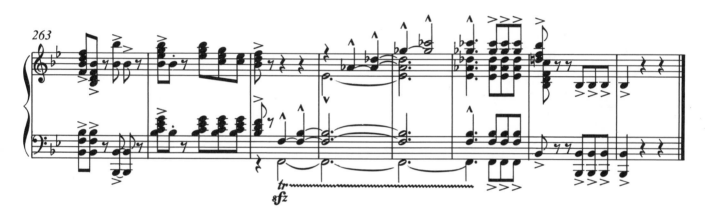

II

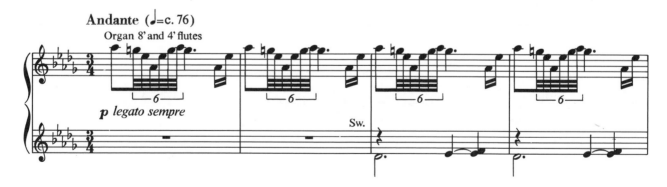

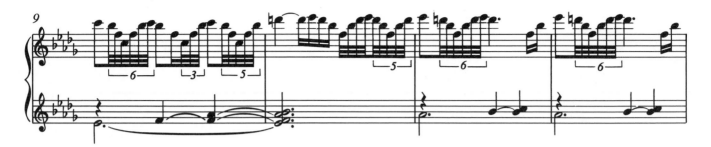

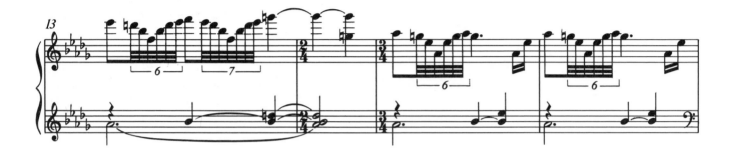

13 TENORS and BASSES

Do-mi - ne De - us, Rex_____ Scae - le-stis,

21 ALTOS

De - us Pa - ter om - ni - po - tens.

TENORS

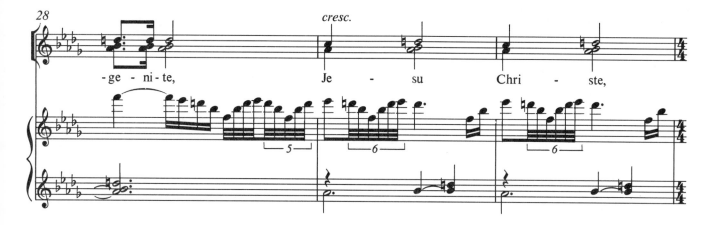

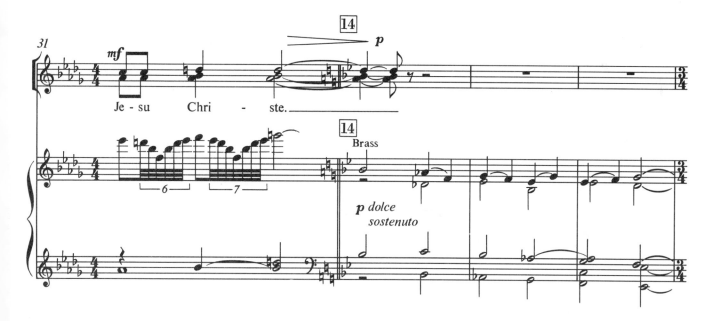

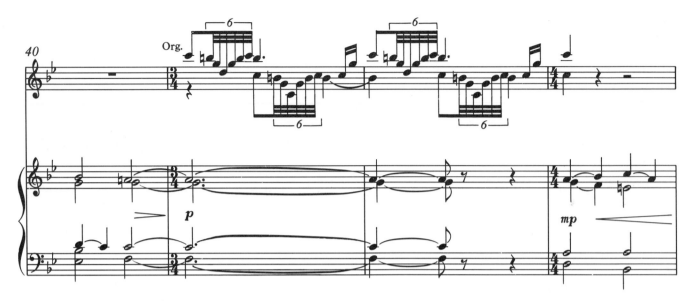

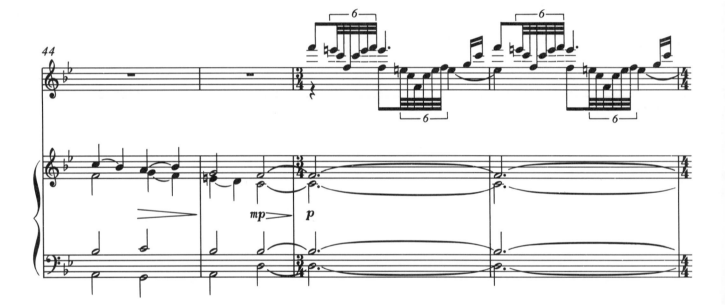

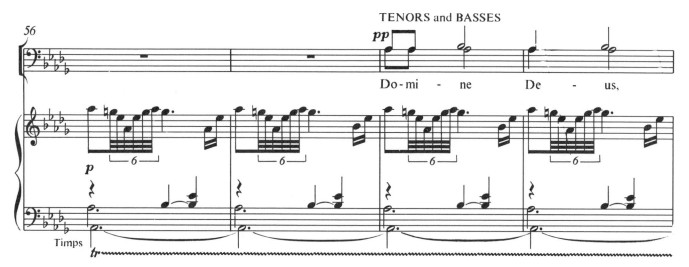

TENORS and BASSES

Do - mi - ne De - us,

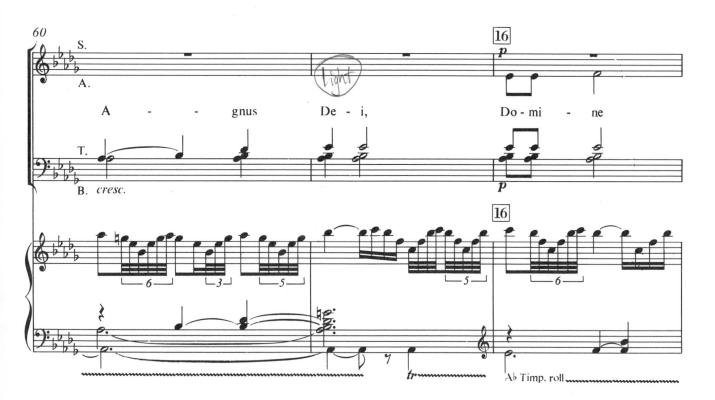

Do - mi - ne

A - gnus De - i,

Do - mi - ne

18

molto legato e tranquillo (♩=76 sempre)

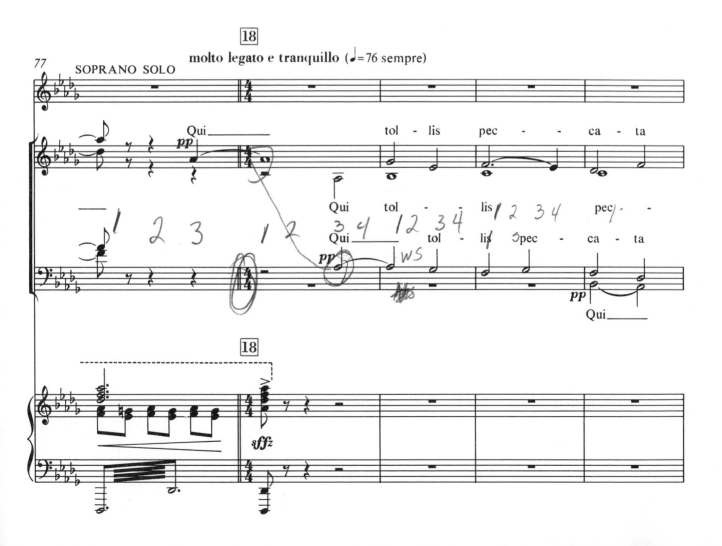

22

III

98

102

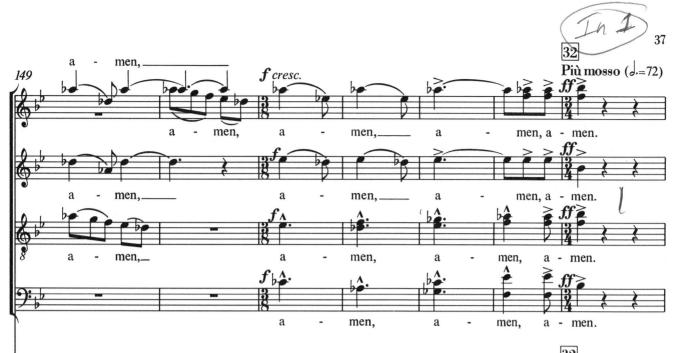

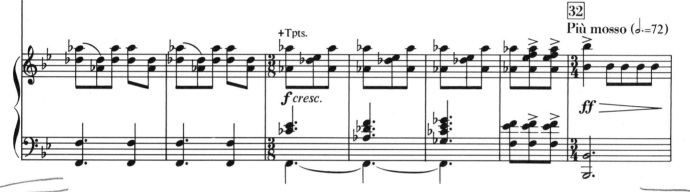

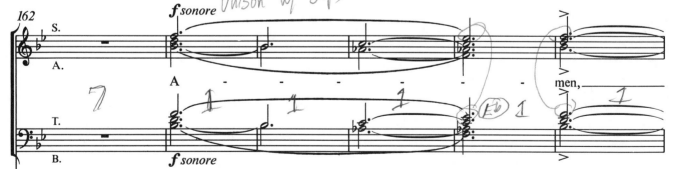

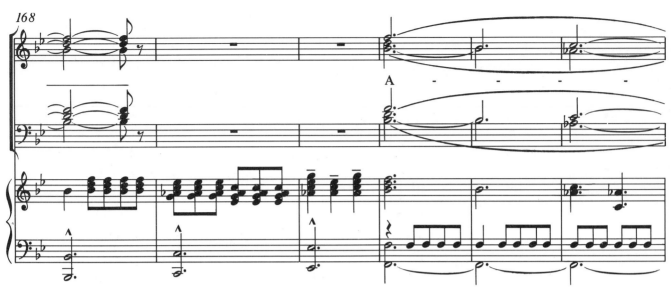

North/So

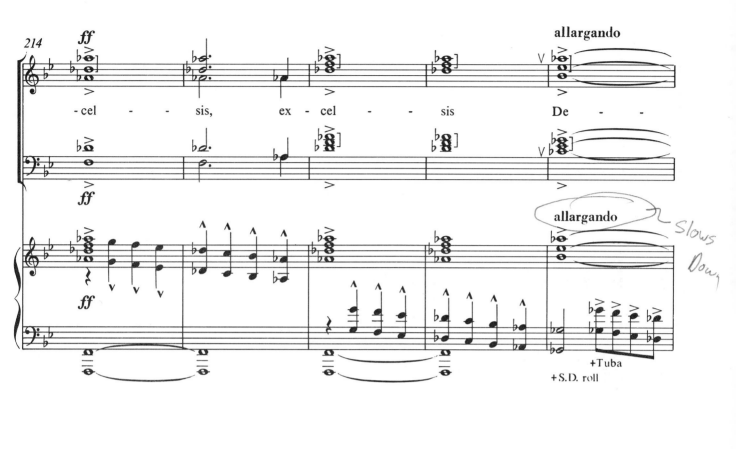